THE UNIVERSE

Earth

Revised and Updated

Stuart Clark

Heinemann Library
Chicago, Illinois

© 2003, 2008 Heinemann Library
a division of Reed Elsevier Inc.
Chicago, Illinois

Customer Service 888-454-2279
Visit our website at www.heinemannraintree.com

Designed by Richard Parker and Manhattan Design
Illustrations by Art Construction
Printed in China by Leo Paper Group

12 11 10 09 08
10 9 8 7 6 5 4 3 2 1

New edition ISBNs: 9781432901639 (hardcover)
                   9781432901752 (paperback)

**The Library of Congress has cataloged the first
edition as follows:**
Clark, Stuart (Stuart G.)
Earth / Stuart Clark.
v. cm. -- (The universe)
Includes bibliographical references and index.
ISBN 1-58810-910-0 (hardcover) -- ISBN 1-40340-611-1 (pbk.)
1. Earth--Juvenile literature. [1. Earth]
 I. Title. II. Series.
QB631.4 .C57 2002
525--dc21
                    2002004060

Acknowledgments
The publishers would like to thank the following for permission to reproduce photographs: Getty Images p. 9; NASA pp. 4, 5; NASA/Shuttle Mission Imagery p. 11; NASA, ESA, M. Robberto (Space Telescope Science Institute/ESA) and the Hubble Space Telescope Orion Treasury Project Team p. 19 Natural History Museum p. 26; Science Photo Library pp. 10, 13, 14, 15, 16, 20, 23 (top and bottom), 24, 25, 27, 28; Still Pictures (Bill O'Connor) p. 29; The Flight Collection p. 12.

Cover photograph reproduced with permission of Science Photo Library/Mike Agliolo.

The publishers would like to thank Geza Gyuk of the Adler Planetarium, Chicago, for his assistance in the preparation of this book.

Contents

Any words appearing in the text in bold, **like this**, are explained in the glossary.

What Does Earth Look Like from Space?

The **planet** we live on is called Earth. From space it looks like a giant, colored ball. Earth is mostly blue because a lot of our planet is covered in water. These are the seas and oceans. The land is colored brown and green and split up into **continents**. The North and South **Poles** are covered in white ice. Clouds drift around Earth.

This picture shows the planet Earth from space.

Our solar system

Earth is one of the eight planets that **orbit** the Sun. Earth is the third planet from the Sun. Mercury and Venus are both closer. Mars, Jupiter, Saturn, Uranus, and Neptune are all farther away. The Sun gives out light and warmth. The closer a planet is to the Sun, the hotter it will be. There are also millions of smaller objects, most only a few miles across, that orbit the Sun. A few of these, the dwarf planets, are up to 1,250 miles (2,000 kilometers) across. Together, the Sun, the planets, and all the smaller objects are called the **solar system**.

This picture shows all eight planets of our solar system, from Mercury to Neptune. Earth is the third planet from the Sun.

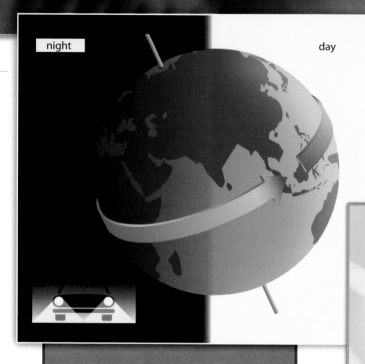

night

day

Because Earth is always spinning on its **axis**, while one side is facing the Sun (and has day) the other is in darkness (and has night).

What shape is Earth?

Earth is shaped like a ball. So are all the other planets. Some ancient people thought Earth was flat and that, if they traveled far enough toward the horizon, they would fall off the edge of the world! Anyone who watched a ship sail away knew this was not true. Instead of falling suddenly, the ship slowly disappeared below the horizon. This proves that Earth's surface slowly curves downward, like the surface of a ball.

Day and night

Standing on Earth, it looks as if the Sun climbs in the sky in the morning, travels across the sky, and drops below the **horizon** at night. In fact, the Sun does not actually move through space. Instead, Earth spins slowly, making it look as if everything moves across the sky. As Earth spins, it shows different sides to the Sun. For the side of Earth facing the Sun, it is daytime. At the same time on the other side of Earth, it is night. It takes 24 hours for Earth to spin around once.

Earth force

Earth has **gravity**. This is the force that keeps us on the ground. Gravity also stops the air we breathe from floating off into space. The **Moon** is caught in the gravity of Earth but is moving so fast that, instead of falling to Earth, it travels around it.

It takes about one month for the Moon to travel around our **planet**. During that time, the Moon always shows us the same face. Dark markings on the Moon are very old **lava** flows from **volcanic eruptions**.

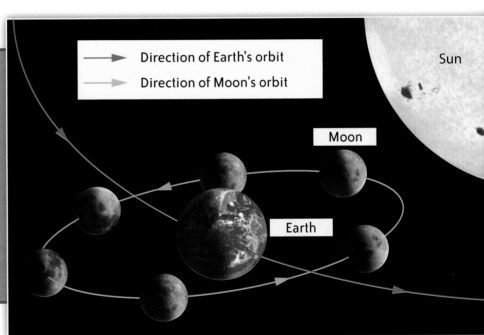

While Earth moves around the Sun, the Moon moves around Earth. Both Earth and the Moon are spinning on their axis at the same time as this.

→ Direction of Earth's orbit

→ Direction of Moon's orbit

Sun

Moon

Earth

How was Earth named?

The word *Earth* comes from **Old English** and German. It was being used before the year 1150. It is the only planet in the **solar system** whose English name is not based on Greek and Roman **mythology**. To the Romans, the Earth goddess was called Tellus, meaning "fertile soil." The Greeks called her Gaia.

Why Does Earth Have Seasons?

Earth follows a circular path around the Sun called an **orbit**. All the other **planets** in the **solar system** also orbit the Sun. It takes Earth one year to travel all the way around its orbit. Depending on Earth's position in its orbit around the Sun, Earth goes through four seasons: spring, summer, fall, and winter.

Going for a spin

As Earth moves through its orbit, it also spins on its **axis**. The axis is an imaginary line that runs from the North **Pole**, through the center of Earth, to the South Pole. Earth's axis is tilted. Instead of pointing straight up, it has been knocked over to the side a little. When the North Pole is leaning toward the Sun, it is summer in the north.

Six months later, Earth has moved half way around its orbit, and the North Pole is now leaning away from the Sun. When this happens, it is winter in the north. When the North Pole is leaning away from the Sun, the South Pole is leaning toward the Sun. So, when it is winter in the north, it is summer in the south.

The seasons change according to Earth's position in its orbit around the Sun.

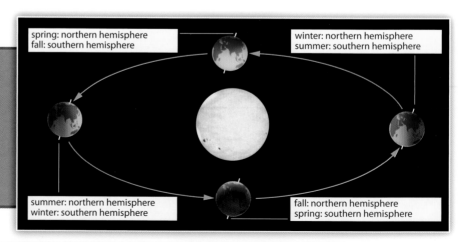

spring: northern hemisphere
fall: southern hemisphere

winter: northern hemisphere
summer: southern hemisphere

summer: northern hemisphere
winter: southern hemisphere

fall: northern hemisphere
spring: southern hemisphere

This series of photos was taken over a period of 24 hours, in Norway, near the Arctic Circle, during the summer. Even at midnight (sixth picture from the left) the Sun does not go below the horizon and, therefore, there is no "night."

Night for six months

During the northern winter and fall, the North Pole is tilted so far away from the Sun that the Sun never rises above the **horizon**. It is night there for six whole months. The same thing happens at the South Pole six months later. When it is spring and summer in the north, the Sun stays in the sky above the North Pole so it is daylight for six whole months. Again, this happens at the South Pole six months later, when it is spring and summer there.

Not all places on Earth have spring, summer, fall, and winter. The **equator** is an imaginary line around the middle of Earth, halfway between the North and South Poles. The area near the equator is known as the **tropics**. In the tropics, it is hot all the time. Some places have a wet season when it rains a lot. At other times of the year, it is very dry. Many deserts are found near the equator. This is where the temperatures are hottest and where there is very little rain.

Why Can We Breathe on Earth?

Earth is covered with a thin blanket of **gases** called the **atmosphere**. The special mixture of gases in Earth's atmosphere is called air. Although many other **planets** have their own atmospheres, no other planet in the **solar system** has an atmosphere with the mixture of gases we call air. So, humans can breathe on Earth, but it would be impossible for us to breathe on the other planets. If astronauts land on other planets, they need to wear spacesuits.

The clouds we see in the sky are part of Earth's atmosphere. If you were standing at the top of one of these mountains in South America, the clouds and mist would be all around you.

Earth's atmosphere

The special gas in the air that we breathe is called oxygen. We need oxygen to change the food we eat into the energy we need to live. Nearly all living things need oxygen to stay alive. Fires need oxygen to burn, too. Not all of our atmosphere is oxygen. Most of it is a gas called nitrogen. Nitrogen puts fires out. If there were more oxygen in our atmosphere and less nitrogen, fires would burn faster and spread more quickly.

The atmosphere is held around Earth by **gravity**. Some planets do not have atmospheres. This is because they are too small to make enough gravity to hold on to the gases. Instead, the gases float off into space.

Astronauts aboard the Space Shuttle *Discovery* recorded this rarely seen moment of a full **Moon** partially obscured by Earth's atmosphere.

How does Earth's atmosphere protect us?

The atmosphere does a lot more than just give us air to breathe. It acts like a blanket, keeping our planet warm. It also blocks out harmful **radiation** from space called cosmic rays. When astronauts spend a long time in space, their spacecraft must have a special room with very thick walls to protect them from cosmic rays. An alarm tells the astronauts when to take shelter because the number of cosmic rays has become dangerous. A special layer in our atmosphere, called the ozone layer, also blocks most of the **ultraviolet light** from the Sun. In small amounts, ultraviolet light will give you a suntan, but large amounts can make people very sick and cause skin cancer.

How High Is the Sky?

What we think of as the sky above our heads is actually Earth's **atmosphere**. The atmosphere stretches about 60 miles (100 kilometers) above the ground. Although that sounds like a lot, it is only about the distance a car travels in an hour. As you get higher up, the atmosphere becomes thinner. This means there are less **gases**, including oxygen, around you. It then gets more difficult to breathe.

This jet is high up in the atmosphere. At this height you can see how Earth's **horizon** curves.

The tallest mountain on Earth is Mount Everest. It rises almost 5.6 miles (9 kilometers) into the sky. At the top of the mountain the air is so thin that most people who climb the mountain have to wear masks to give them extra oxygen so that they can breathe.

Flying above the clouds

Jet aircraft fly at about 6 miles (10 kilometers) above the ground. This is the highest that people can travel, unless they are astronauts going into space. Most clouds form between about 1.5 miles (2 kilometers) and 3 miles (5 kilometers) above the ground. There are many different types of cloud, and scientists study them to help predict the weather.

Burn up

Entering Earth's atmosphere can make things burn up. Sometimes bright darts of light shoot across the sky. These are called shooting stars, but they are not really stars. They are tiny pieces of space dust coming toward Earth. They fly through space very quickly. When they hit the atmosphere, they become very hot and burn up because of friction. Friction is what makes your hands warm when you rub them together.

This artwork shows how the Space Shuttle does not burn up when it re-enters the atmosphere because it is covered in heat-proof tiles.

Spacecraft

The lowest spacecraft **orbit** Earth at 322 miles (515 kilometers). Sometimes Earth's **gravity** pulls them down. Like shooting stars, they hit the atmosphere and burn up. In 2001 the Russian space program destroyed its old **space station**, called Mir, in this way. They used a spacecraft to push it into a **collision course** with Earth's atmosphere. The heat burned up most of the space station, but not all of it. It was so big that some of it survived and fell into the Pacific Ocean.

What Is Earth's Surface Like?

Land and oceans cover Earth's surface. There are many different types of land. Some parts are covered with jungles, others with snow. There are rugged mountains and hot, sandy deserts.

Earth has all sorts of weather. Storms in the **tropics** have very strong winds and produce huge amounts of rain.

The oceans are very special. They are Earth's central heating system. They help warm up the cooler parts of the **planet**. In some houses, hot water is pumped around the radiators to keep the rooms warm. On Earth, warm water moves around the oceans, keeping some countries warmer than others.

The right distance from the Sun

Earth is very different from all the other planets in the **solar system**. It is the only one that has animals and plants living on it. This is because our planet is just the right distance from the Sun.

If Earth were closer to the Sun, it would be so hot that the water would boil away. If Earth were too far away from the Sun, it would be so cold that the oceans would freeze into solid ice. Without water, life on Earth would be impossible.

Factories and power stations that burn **fossil fuels** are adding to the pollution in our atmosphere.

Is Earth's climate changing?

Scientists are now very worried that Earth's **climate** is changing. For more than 20 years, Earth has been getting hotter. Part of this change is natural. Throughout Earth's history temperatures have been changing slightly. However, some of the present change is being caused by pollution. This is waste **gas** from cars and factories. The pollution hangs in the **atmosphere** and acts like a blanket on a bed, keeping in heat. If we continue to cause air pollution, Earth will become too hot for us to live.

What Is Earth Made Of?

Earth is made mostly of rocks. The rocks are made of many different **chemicals**. Scientists called **geologists** study rocks. When geologists know what a rock is made of, they can figure out how it was formed. There are three different types of rock on Earth. These rocks make up the surface. The surface of Earth is called the **crust** and is usually between 6 and 30 miles (10 and 50 kilometers) thick. In some places under the oceans, it can be much thinner.

Different layers

The first type of rock is called **igneous rock**. This makes up most of Earth's surface and was once **molten lava**. The lava **erupts** from **volcanoes** and then cools down to become rock. The second type of rock is called **sedimentary rock**. This is made of little bits of sand and other small pieces that drift to the bottom of the sea. As more bits fall on top, the tiny pieces are crushed together and become rock. The third type is called **metamorphic rock**. This is made from igneous or sedimentary rocks that have been squeezed or heated inside Earth and turned into different rocks.

You can see the different layers in this sedimentary rock along the coast of the Isle of Wight, in the United Kingdom.

Inside Earth

Geologists can use special equipment to listen to sounds traveling through Earth. It is a good way to discover far away **earthquakes** and **volcanic eruptions**. This process is called **seismology**. It also helps scientists discover what is inside Earth. When scientists first listened to the inside of Earth, they found that at the very center of our **planet** there is a large ball of metal, or a core. It is mostly made of iron and nickel. At the surface of the ball, the metal is molten, but near the center the pressure is so great that it is solid.

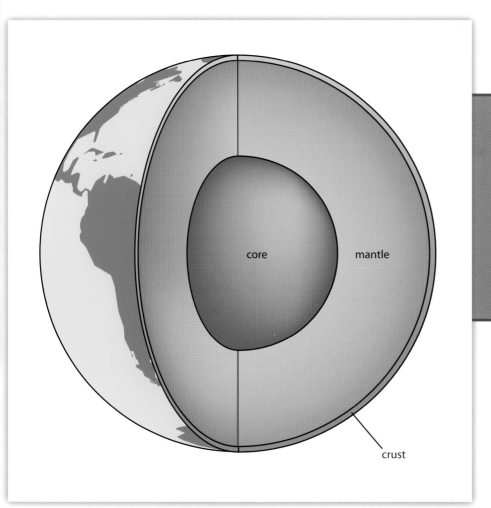

Inside Earth there are different regions of rock (the crust and mantle) and metal (the core).

How Was Earth Made?

Geologists are very good at measuring the different types of chemicals that make up the rocks on Earth. By weighing the amount of each chemical inside a rock, scientists can measure how old it is. Using this method to find the oldest rocks on Earth, geologists have figured out that Earth is 4.5 billion years old. A big clue about how Earth was actually formed can be found in space.

Astronomers have figured out that the Sun is also 4.5 billion years old. This tells us that Earth, the Sun, and all the planets formed at the same time.

Clouds in space

When astronomers look into space, they see enormous clouds of gas and dust. Some of the clouds reflect light, giving off beautiful red, yellow, and green colors. The clouds are much bigger than planets or stars. Using telescopes to look inside them, astronomers can see that stars form inside these clouds. Planets must form inside them, too.

Star making

As the clouds float through space, gravity pulls parts of them closer together. This is the first step in making a star. As the gas is squeezed together by gravity, it heats up and becomes a star. Small clouds of dust then form around these very young stars. This is where astronomers think planets form. So, stars and planets form together, at the same time, and this is how scientists think our solar system was made.

Planets forming

No one has ever seen a planet forming. Telescopes are not powerful enough to see any detail in the dusty clouds that surround young stars. Astronomers are working to build bigger telescopes that will see into the clouds. Until those telescopes are finished, astronomers have to rely on very powerful computers to help them calculate what happens when a planet forms. They believe it takes many millions of years for a planet to form completely.

Astronomers' calculations tell them that the dust in the cloud begins to stick together. This takes a long time. After many, many thousands of years, the dust sticks together to make rocks. Then, the rocks start to bump into each other. When this happens, they melt and stick together. As more of the rocks stick together, they form planets, and this is how scientists think Earth was made.

This crater is in Arizona. It is huge—2,600 feet (800 meters) wide and 650 feet (200 meters) deep.

Craters

Over millions of years, many rocks have come together in space to form **planets**, but there are still some rocks that have not. The **craters** on the **Moon** were caused as these last pieces of rock were caught by **gravity** and crashed into the Moon's surface. There would be many craters on Earth, too, but most of them have been worn away by the weather.

The restless Earth

Even today, the temperature inside Earth is high, and some of the rocks are still **molten**. This is called **magma**, and it behaves like a liquid. The surface of Earth is not one solid **crust**. Instead it is broken into large pieces called plates. The plates hold the **continents** and the oceans and they float on the magma. As the liquid magma moves, so do the plates. Sometimes they collide. Other times they pull apart. When plates rub along each other, **earthquakes** happen. These shake the ground and cause awful damage. The plate containing the Pacific Ocean rubs against the west coast of the United States, creating terrible earthquakes from time to time. If continents collide, the plates can push up into mountain ranges. This is happening at the moment where India is pushing into Asia, creating the Himalayan mountain range.

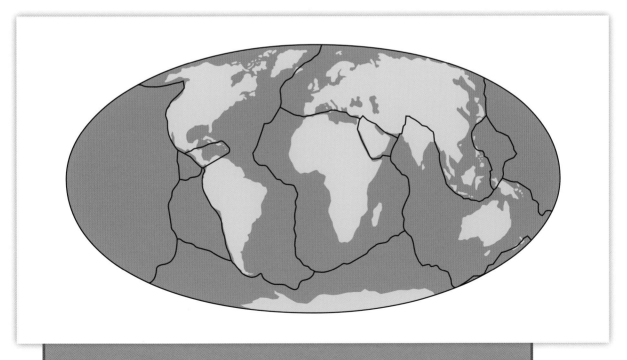

Earth's crust fits together like a jigsaw puzzle. The pieces are called plates. Wherever two plates meet or touch, there is a risk of earthquakes.

One enormous continent

Most of the land on Earth was once a single, enormous **continent**. It split apart 250 million years ago, and the pieces have taken all of that time to drift into their present positions. South America looks as though it would fit into Africa like a jigsaw puzzle because once, long ago, they were joined together.

Volcanic eruptions

Magma can also rise to the surface of Earth and **erupt** through holes that become **volcanoes**. When magma flows out of Earth it is called **lava**. As it hardens and turns into new rock, it builds large volcanoes.

This is what Earth would have looked like 250 million years ago. You can see the huge continents Eurasia, Laurentia, and Gondwana. Also labeled here are the names of some of the continents and countries as they are known today.

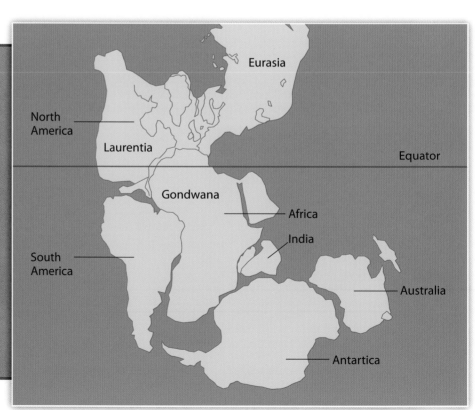

It is very difficult to know when a volcano will erupt. There can be many years or even decades between **volcanic eruptions**.
A volcano is said to be dormant when it is not erupting. When it stops erupting altogether, a volcano is said to be extinct.

Some volcanos erupt violently, with explosions and huge clouds of ash. Others erupt gently, with flowing lava and no explosions.

Changing Earth

There were times in the past when Earth was much colder than it is today. These times are called ice ages. Huge sheets of ice crept over the land and gigantic icebergs floated on the oceans. Ice ages may be caused when extremely large volcanoes erupt. They throw clouds of ash into the **atmosphere** and stop sunlight from reaching Earth. The temperature of our **planet** would then drop and an ice age would happen.

When Did Life Begin on Earth?

Fossils are made when parts of dead animals or plants leave marks in **sedimentary rocks**. Scientists have found very old fossils in some rocks. These fossils are amazing because they are not like the large bones of dinosaurs. Instead, they are very tiny fossils of **bacteria**. These are the smallest life forms found on Earth and can only be seen through a microscope. There are many different types of bacteria. Today, some bacteria give us illnesses, while others live inside us and help us to digest our food. The rocks in which fossils of old bacteria have been found are 3.5 billion years old.

Some of these ammonite fossils are around 380 million years old. Ammonites were a type of sea snail.

Scientists have found rocks almost four billion years old that were probably made from dead bacteria. So, it seems that bacteria were the first life forms on Earth. No one knows exactly how bacteria formed in the first place. This is one of the most puzzling questions in modern science.

Plants and animals

For nearly three billion years, bacteria were the only kind of life that lived on Earth, and they were only found in the oceans. Then, 600 million years ago, life on Earth suddenly changed. Groups of bacteria stuck together and worked together, becoming more complicated. Plants and animals developed. The first plants were like vines and the first animals were like jellyfish. Eventually both plants and animals found ways to leave the ocean and to live on the land.

Mass extinction

Animals and plants change all the time. Usually they become more and more complicated. This change is called evolution, and it means that animals and plants can adapt to new situations. One mystery that remains to be solved by scientists is why certain types of animals die out suddenly. When this happens it is called a **mass extinction**. There have been five mass extinctions during Earth's history.

Simple creatures, such as this jellyfish, were some of the first animals to develop on Earth.

This Shunosaurus dinosaur skeleton was found in China. The Shunosaurus was a plant-eating dinosaur, so even if it had survived the impact of the asteroid, it would probably have starved with no plants left to eat.

Death of the dinosaurs

A very important **mass extinction** took place 65 million years ago. This was when the last of the dinosaurs died out suddenly. The dinosaurs were giant animals that lived on Earth between 65 and 225 million years ago. Most scientists believe that they were finally wiped out when a gigantic lump of space rock, known as an **asteroid**, hit Earth. If an asteroid the size of a mountain (a few miles or larger) crashes into a **planet**, it will make a very large **crater**, start fires all across the world, and throw huge amounts of dust up into the **atmosphere**. The dust blocks most of the sunlight and causes the plants and the animals that eat them to die. These terrible disasters probably killed the dinosaurs and a large number of other animals and plants. Scientists have found evidence that other mass extinctions may also have been caused by asteroids.

The birth of man

The extinction of the dinosaurs is important to us because, after the death of these huge creatures, there was more food for the smaller creatures called **mammals**. Mammals began to **evolve** about 210 million years ago. They give birth to live babies rather than laying eggs. They also feed their babies with milk. Humans are highly developed mammals. Scientists believe that humans evolved from earlier, simpler mammals. The first mammals evolved to become more complicated and more intelligent. After millions of years they finally became human beings.

This is an artist's idea of what early humans would have looked like around one million years ago.

Changing Earth

There is always a small risk that another asteroid might hit Earth. **Astronomers** are building new telescopes and searching the skies for dangerous asteroids. If such an asteroid is discovered, instead of blowing it up, scientists will try to push it into a new **orbit** so that it will not crash into Earth.

Fact File

Here are some interesting facts about Earth:

Length of day: 24 hours

Distance from Sun: 93 million miles (150 million kilometers)

Time to go around the Sun: 365.25 days (So, every fourth year we have to include an extra day in the calendar, February 29. These years are known as leap years. If we did not do this, the seasons would shift out of order with the months of the year.)

Size: Earth is 7,968 miles (12,750 kilometers) across

Surface area: The surface of Earth measures 196 million square miles (510 million square kilometers)

Average height of the land: 2,750 feet (840 meters) above sea level

Average depth of the oceans: 12,470 feet (3,800 meters)

While one half of Earth is in sunlight and has day, the other half is in darkness and has night.

Earth's **atmosphere** is made of:

Nitrogen **gas**	78 percent
Oxygen gas	21 percent
Argon gas	0.9 percent
All other gases	0.1 percent

The five longest rivers:

Nile	4,145 miles (6,670 kilometers)
Amazon	4,000 miles (6,430 kilometers)
Yangtze	3,915 miles (6,300 kilometers)
Mississippi	3,741 miles (6,020 kilometers)
Yenisei-Angara	3,442 miles (5,540 kilometers)

The Himalayan mountain range is the highest in the world. It is constantly covered in snow, and nothing lives on the mountain peaks.

The five tallest mountains:

Mount Everest	5.5 miles (8.8 kilometers)
Godwin Austen (K2)	5.4 miles (8.6 kilometers)
Kanchenjunga	5.33 miles (8.59 kilometers)
Lhotse	5.3 miles (8.5 kilometers)
Makalu	5.3 miles (8.5 kilometers)

Glossary

asteroid small object orbiting the Sun. Some are just lumps of rock in space. Others are many miles wide.

astronomer scientist who studies space, planets, and stars

atmosphere blanket of gas around a planet or moon

axis imaginary line that a planet spins around

bacteria tiny, basic life forms

chemical substance that everything is made up from

climate weather conditions

collision course about to hit or crash into something

continent very large piece of land on Earth. North America is a continent.

crater large, bowl-shaped hole in the surface of a planet or moon caused by an asteroid crashing into it

crust outer layer of Earth. All the continents and oceans sit on the crust.

earthquake when the surface of Earth moves suddenly

equator imaginary line around the middle of Earth

erupt burst out

evolve change over time

fossil fuel natural fuel such as coal, oil, and gas

gas substance such as air

geologist scientist who studies rocks

gravity force that pulls all objects toward the surface of Earth or any other planet, moon, or star

horizon line where the land and the sky seem to meet

igneous rock rock made from lava

lava liquid rock that erupts from volcanoes

magma rocks that are so hot they are liquid and runny

mammal animal that gives birth to babies and feeds them with milk. Humans are mammals.

mass extinction when a type of animal dies out forever

metamorphic rock rock changed by heat or squeezing

molten something that has been melted

Moon, the natural satellite that orbits Earth. Astronauts first went there in 1969.

mythology old stories, told to explain how something came to be

Old English language people in England used to speak before the year 1150. It is different from the English spoken now.

orbit path one object takes around another

planet large object that orbits a star. Earth is a planet.

pole point due north or south that marks the end of an invisible line, called the axis, about which a planet, moon, or star spins

radiation energy rays from the Sun

sedimentary rock rock made up over time from tiny bits

seismology special way of listening for, and studying, earthquakes

solar system all the planets, moons, asteroids, and comets around the Sun

space station large man-made object that orbits Earth. Astronauts can live on it.

tropics area of Earth around the equator

ultraviolet light special light that cannot be seen by humans. Ultraviolet light from the Sun causes skin to tan and can cause cancer.

volcanic eruption active volcano that spills lava on to Earth's surface

volcano opening in a planet's surface through which hot, liquid rock is thrown up

More Books to Read

Chancellor, Deborah. *Planet Earth*. Boston: Kingfisher, 2006.

Kerrod, Robin. *Eyewitness Guides: Universe*. New York: Dorling Kindersley, 2003.

Riley, Peter D. *The Earth in Space*. New York: Franklin Watts, 2003.

Index